Airbnb Beginner's Guide to Hosting

How To Set Up And Run Your Own Airbnb Business

Lauren Coats

Copyright © 2018 Lauren Coats

All rights reserved.

ISBN 13: 978-1-72-684520-5

DEDICATION

I dedicate this book to my one true love, my late Chihuahua, Siralina. She was by my side while I wrote this book and built my Airbnb career, encouraging me and inspiring me each and every day to be a better dog mom, Host, and human. She was my soul mate, best companion, my angel and my light. I miss you dearly Chookie, my Teeny Tiny Love.

CONTENTS

	Acknowledgements	i
	Introduction	8
1	Becoming an Airbnb Host	10
2	Setting Up Your Space!	13
3	Linens, Bedding, Supplies and Supply Closet	17
4	Creating The Listing	22
5	Cleaning Logistics	30
6	Hosting	41
7	Set Up Supply Lists	49
8	House Manual and Local Food Guide Example	57
9	Cleaners Checklist	70

ACKNOWLEDGMENTS

I would like to thank all my Airbnb Guests, you are a blessing and have given my life great purpose. Thank you to my friends and family who support me, love me, and encourage me to share my Hosting knowledge with the world.

INTRODUCTION

The Importance Of Traveling And Hosting

"To travel the world is to meet your soul." -Lauren Coats

"A wise man travels to discover himself." -James Russell Lowell

"To travel is to take a journey into yourself." -Danny Kaye

"Travel far enough, you meet yourself." -David Mitchell

"Travel is the only thing you buy that makes you richer." -Unknown

World traveling is a huge mind expander, whether you are a Western person visiting a third world country for the first time, or just a curious explorer flying into a new city. Each new culture, new experience, new exploration takes us one step closer to getting to know who we are. The way we react, love, give, share or don't share when put into a new culture teaches us so much about ourselves and our conditioning. As you travel more and more, you find and observe overlapping patterns of self-behavior, and you see others react positively or negatively to who you 'really' are – the part of you that translates to everyone you meet.

When we host travelers, we are giving an ultimate gift. We are hosting a seeker, an explorer, a human being that has sacrificed and worked hard for this time of leisure, exploring, unwinding, relaxing or to have fun. This is a sacred time of self healing and life changing experiences, and it should be honored and respected with grand importance. We all are running around, in chaos, chasing our survival. When we take a break with ourselves, partner, family or friends to make a trip, we are getting back to who we are without the stress and burdens of everyday life. We re-set, re-charge, and re-connect to ourselves.

I encourage you to host your guests with the utmost love and respect. This is a service that you are providing that changes lives – you are giving a safe, warm, cozy place to relax and unwind during their holiday or work trip. You are offering a secure place for rest in an unknown and sometimes intimidating new place. You can be proud and fulfilled by giving this gift of service to others. Every ounce of energy you spend making your space comfortable, beautiful, clean and ready is an offering you are making to the healing and growing of all humanity. Tired travelers are the norm, so being hospitable and gracious is your responsibility.

By hosting your own Airbnb, you are going to be working for yourself. You are your own boss. You decide how your life is going to roll and what it is going to look like. You decide your schedule, your work hours, your employee's, the whole design, essence and energy of the space and experience. This is personal power and freedom. You are also creating jobs for others (your cleaner, handyman, co-hosts), a precious gift. You have the chance to be the boss you always wanted to have. You can be independent of the 9-5 system and corporate slavery. You are leading the way for people to travel in style and comfort and expand their minds. Good on you! Never forget, the work you do changes lives and makes or breaks the $1000's of dollars investment your guest made for their well deserved vacation.

I am overjoyed with my work, I love to take care of my guests, check on them, upgrade my spaces with nicer art, decorations and appliances as I can. I care that they enjoy my place, that they can relax there, re-charge, have a positive experience and grow as human beings.

CHAPTER 1

Becoming An Airbnb Host

Some things to consider before investing and committing to the Host role...

1. 24/7 Online Lifestyle

You will be playing a Vacation Rental Property Management role, which is a 24/7 commitment. As an all-star Host, you will have someone be available to your guests last minute and semi-around the clock. Sometimes guests will lock themselves out at 11pm and request the host come over right away with a spare key, one afternoon a hot water heater may break and you will spend the whole day meeting handymen and handling the repair. You can also explain to your guests your soonest availability, and try to accommodate them with a healthy balance for your lifestyle and other responsibilities. I have been at social events having a great time, only to have to leave for an Airbnb emergency. To have designated off-hours, you'll need to hire a co-host to be on duty when you're offline.

In the "Interactions with Guests" section of your listing, you can set the expectations for guest communication and your availability. If you choose to be more hands off, an example for your listing would be, "My full-time job and family schedule keep me pretty busy, so I will try to make myself available to you when needed but I have other obligations as well." This sounds ok! I personally say "I am on Airbnb messenger a few times a day, but texts to my cell are the quickest way to reach me." As I run many properties, I must be online any way, so I choose to make myself very available to my guests.

In general, guests want to be well taken care of and feel that your top priority is their comfort. I look at my phone every 3-4 hours just to make sure an Airbnb situation hasn't gotten out of control out of nowhere. My week long, disconnected, offline camping trips will have to happen after my Airbnb Host career ends, or I hire a very proficient co-host. Yes, you can hire someone to run your Airbnb App and take phone calls, but every detail and nuance of protocol for certain issues is hard to train someone on if you have multiple properties for different clients, as there is a sensitivity to handle everything correctly to ensure positive guest reviews and positive client, owner, landlord relations. Can you trust your friend/employee to handle every situation with elegance, grace, and maximum hospitality/problem solving skills?

2. Committing to be an Amazing Host

To be a fantastic Host, and therefore make fantastic money, you must have the Hosting Trifecta: excellent communication skills + incredible cleaning team + a smooth check in/check out process for your guests. Responding to guest questions, concerns, and extra requests with speed, care, and detailed accuracy are important, and making sure the guests have checked in without delay or frustration are important communication responsibilities. Lock boxes for check in are a Host's best friend. I set up an 'emergency' lock box hidden in another accessible area in case the guest looses their keys. If needed I send them the lock box code for the spare key and save myself an inconvenient, last minute trip to the property. You will need your cleaners to be reliable, make themselves available to you, have great attention to detail, and be able to follow your instructions.

3. Time and Financial Investment

If you are setting up an Airbnb from scratch in an empty house, you have quite a task ahead of you. Depending on your budget, availability, and the team you have to assist you, it could take a month from start to finish. Buying all supplies, furnishing the home, decorating, photographing, making your listing, and doing competition research to price your home accordingly, it is a long list of tasks.

In general, it will cost a minimum of $2000-$10,000 to set up an Airbnb from scratch. It could be the first months rent + security deposit, purchasing all the necessary items and furniture, paying workers to help move furniture, and utility bills. Bedding alone can easily cost $500+. Be aware it could take a few months to make back your initial investment. If the market is good for Airbnb rentals in your area and you have done the basic calculations of your expenses, time investment, financial investment, achievable price per night and profit margin, you could have just started an amazing small business with plenty of room for growth. If the price per night and monthly income from your bookings will not cover your expenses, you may want to re-think your new Airbnb project.

CHAPTER 2

Setting Up Your Space!

How exciting. You have a new space where the local government, owner and/or landlord has given you permission to do Airbnb, maybe you've just bought a new investment property, or you'll be welcoming guests into in your own home. Now its time to set it up!

What is the vibe or feeling you want your space to have? What is your budget for all the supplies, furniture and decorations? Do you have an SUV or truck for picking up furniture? With this information you will develop a buying strategy for your new supplies.

In this chapter, we will cover buying strategies, furniture, decor, linens and bedding, kitchen appliances, bathroom items, cleaning supplies, and creating a locked supply closet.

What is a Buying Strategy? It is the method and retail shops/online forums you will buy your supplies from according to your timeline and budget. Ikea, Amazon, Craigslist, Overstock.com, Wal-Mart, second hand shops/thrift stores, Big Lots, Home Goods, dollar stores, Goodwill, Marshalls, etc are great resources for furnishing your new Airbnb (most of these recommendations are American over-stock retail stores, selling brand new, brand names for 40-60% less than department stores. You may have an equivalent available in your country).

What is your timeline and budget? Depending on your answer, you will buy things quicker for convenience or have more time to shop around for better prices and designs. Maybe you will need to hire someone and rent a U-Haul truck (American company specializing in moving truck rentals) for moving furniture, so you will want to coordinate all of your furniture buying/moving on those days.

Developing your own Buying Strategy: Make a list of all the items you need to buy, you can reference the "Supply List" in the following chapter for an overview of everything you will need for each room. Bedding can be purchased quickly through Amazon. For all other items, go to the store's you like best first, and buy the cooler, nicer, design items at an affordable cost. You can peruse second hand shops, Home Goods, Big Lots, Marshalls, Ikea, etc for these items (or any discount retail store). If you don't find what you love and what's affordable during these exploring trips, head over to Wal-Mart as your last stop to buy everything you couldn't find elsewhere. If you don't find it there, go back on Amazon for convenience and speed. An Amazon prime membership will come in handy throughout your hosting career.

Furnishing Your Space: Purchasing, Assembly, Furniture Positions

Purchasing Furniture: There are many different places to buy furniture. Free Craigslist, paid Craigslist, yard sales, Amazon, Alibaba.com, Ikea, thrift shops, secondhand furniture shops, Overstock.com, NextDoor App, Letgo.com, Goodwill, Offerup.com, any second hand websites available in your country. Many items you can also buy new from cheap discount stores like Wal-Mart or Big Lots.

Assembling Furniture: I resist furnishing the entire home with Ikea goods, as I don't have the patience for assembly and following the detailed instructions. I usually hire a friend to do it, but at $15/hour it takes my friends so long that I could have bought something nicer I liked better with the money I paid for them to put it together. I created a job, this is positive, but Ikea furniture can be mega-intense if you are using it on the entire place. Keep assembly in mind when buying large amounts of new furniture.

Furniture Positions: Move around your couch, carpets, chairs, dining table, coffee table, and armoire's for best decorative value and spacious living. Try more than one set up, take photos and ask your friends what they think. If you have an aesthetically sensitive friend with good taste, invite them over and have them critique your furniture position ideas. Just because your friend, partner, or family member suggests a particular furniture set up, do what feels right to you. You can also view the photographs and make a decision based on how they look and feel.

Decorating the Space: Goals, Feel, Title, Artwork, Home Décor Items

The home décor areas of Ikea, Wal-Mart, Costco, Ross, Marshalls, Amazon, Home Goods, World Market, and your local dollar store are incredible places to find decorations. I like to use succulents in a cute pot (low maintenance), candle sets, fake plants in beautiful pots, little statues, colorful books, and rocks/shells as they are great home décor items for Airbnb's. A decorative mirror in each room is a great way to fill up your space and easy to coordinate with the furniture and artwork.

Décor Goals: When you look at the furniture you have, the location of your property, and the amenities you offer, you can think about what your goals are for the space. What are its best attributes and how can you enhance them? Do you have an excellent patio? Fill it with plants and a relaxing patio table and chairs, photograph it, and then highlight it in your listing as a zen morning coffee space or romantic evening wine table. Great view? Make that your featured photo and decorate the space around it. Mountain cabin? You can decorate your place to accent the marketable, unique features, and have your space integrated into its fullest potential.

Theme: Is your home beach-y, neutral and family friendly, clean and minimal, modern and elegant, bohemian/kitschy/eclectic, or a hotel-style, business friendly place? What kind of environment and experience do you want to create? What design and aesthetics do you want to have? Do you want to cater to business men, couples, large families, younger people? All these groups? This is possible. Setting goals and thinking about what kind of style you want for your space will guide your purchases along the way. Maybe you are on a very tight budget and using free or available second hand furniture, no problem! See what you can piece together by buying artwork or decorative pillows to tie your odds and ends together.

Feel: How do you want your space to feel? Cozy and homey, modern and chic, minimal and grey, colorful and artistic, relaxing and zen, spacious and neutral, you must ask yourself what is the feel of your home, as this will guide your purchasing, decorating, and also help you to describe your space when you create your Airbnb listing.

Title: The title for your Airbnb listing should accentuate its best qualities. You have an ocean view? Very easy – your title should shout Ocean View. Great neighborhood? Put it in the title. Quiet and private, cozy and sunny, spacious and charming, antique or retro? Highlight the best features you are offering in your title.

My Airbnb's are in Hollywood and every title starts with it. Location, vibe, stand out qualities, major benefits (quiet, large, cozy, comfortable) or even something unique you offer. You can try out more eccentric titles and see how it goes. On my personal home I had a funky Spanish title and didn't get any bookings, so I changed it to something more neutral and right away it was booked solid (it had Hollywood in it)! You may want to appeal to the masses, or a niche group, both are valuable strategies.

Artwork: Artwork can be a very expensive and a subjective topic. I always recommend one or two paintings in each room that work well together and a large decorative mirror on the other wall. Decorative mirrors are a less expensive and useful item to fill wall space. I like to buy artwork first that goes with my furniture and then buy complimentary decorative mirrors, and then items for the coffee tables, counters, bed side tables, and bathroom vanities. I use mirrors between 1.5'-2.5' x 2'-3'. You can also hang it on top of a dresser for a vanity feel in the bedrooms.

Home Décor Items: There are many elegant, simple and chic items you can place on coffee tables, bedside tables, kitchen shelves, bathroom shelves, to add a homey feeling and 'fill out' the space. Little statues, succulent plants, little boxes, picture frames with nice nature photos or inspiring quotes, candle sets, books, fake plants are a few examples.

Without home décor items, your place could feel barren and not lived in. I like to use upscale and tasteful fake plants. They are not easy to find, you will find a lot of plastic/rubber looking fake plants. I put a decorative candle holder and candle almost everywhere. There is a small risk for fire, but I have not had any issues so far. Buying inexpensive books at Goodwill or thrift stores for fifty cents to $2 to fill up a book shelf, coffee table, or the bedroom shelves is a great move. In general, Goodwill is a great place to pick up inexpensive decorative items for the home.

CHAPTER 3

Linens, Bedding, Supplies and Supply Closet

Purchasing, Bedding Sets, Cleaning Times, Bathroom, Kitchen, Cleaning Supplies, Supply Closet

Purchasing Bedding: I suggest to buy microfiber linens online. They resist stains, lint, and wrinkles (wrinkles are a huge issue with bedding – you will not want to pay a cleaner to iron all your sheets and duvets). I buy from Amazon, they have an incredible assortment of microfiber options, and in-store bedding can be much more expensive. Medium shades are recommended as they do not show stains or lint very much. White/light colors will stain, and dark colors will show lint dramatically. Practical, long lasting color choices would medium grey, medium blue, darker gray, teal, purple colors. If you choose to go with white, expect to replace your bedding often due to stains.

Heavy duty and ribbed towels are highly recommended, as your towels will be washed an incredible amount, and little threads can come loose and pull, and then the towel looks old and needs to be replaced. Ribbed towels hides these imperfections. I recommend stocking at least one extra towel for guests. For example, if you have 4 guests, provide 5 towels. You can also provide the same amount of towels every time, regardless of your guest count, to keep track of your bedding inventory easily and charge the guests for missing towels. If you live near a beach, river, lake or other swimming area, I suggest providing separate beach/outdoor towels, as your guests will take your bath towels there.

Bedding Sets and Cleaning Times: Bedding is a key aspect to running your Airbnb smoothly. There are complicated logistics to be worked out here depending on how many properties you have. As standard checkout/check-in times give about a four hour window for the cleaners to prepare the home (11am check out, 3pm check in), your cleaning team may be done cleaning and in and out in one or two hours. They will not have enough time to do all the laundry on site (2-3 loads = 3-4 hours). If you have one cleaner coming in to clean, it may take them 2-3 hours to clean, but you will have to pay them to wait for the laundry to be ready (upwards of 3.5-4 hours for everything to dry and be ready). If you have 2-4 checkouts in one day, doing all the laundry on site is impossible.

Solution? Create bedding 'sets.' This is an extra clean full set of bedding for the entire home. Fitted sheets, flat sheets, duvet covers, pillow cases, towels, hand towels, wash clothes and bathmats. With extra bedding sets, the cleaners can enter, clean, change the bedding, and move on to the next apartment or be finished quickly. They could also start the laundry while cleaning, and keep that going at each place. Wash a load at one home, take it with them wet and dry it at the next. Cleaners will then do the rest of the dirty laundry at home on their own time.

The amount of time needed to do three loads of laundry is an average of 3 hours (depending on your machines). If a cleaning team needs to clean three apartments in four hours, and it takes 3 hours to do all the laundry per place, that's 12 hours of laundry. You will have to work out the payment arrangement (flat fee per job or hourly) for your cleaner to incorporate doing the laundry at home. Sometimes one cleaner will pick up the laundry from each home, go to the Laundromat, and then return each clean set to each apartment. This will be 2-4 hours of work, plus the cost of the Laundromat. I don't recommend this system. It is an expensive investment to order duplicate bedding sets, but you will save time and money in the long term allowing your cleaners to do laundry in their off-time. You will want your cleaning team to have a car and machines at home to transport and do the laundry easily without visiting Laundromats.

My best recommendation is to purchase enough extra bedding 'sets' so the cleaner can move quickly and turn over all needed apartments without being delayed by the laundry. You will also want to consider having universal bedding/towels for all your places, so the bedding is the same and interchangeable for all your Airbnb's. If you choose to do home specific bedding, you may need to have more than one set of duplicate bedding, as different cleaners may be cleaning on different days. For example, Molly cleans apartment 1 on Tuesday. On Thursday, Mary is set to clean apartment 1. Will she have to drive across town to pick up the clean bedding from Molly? This will add 1-2 hours to her cleaning process, therefore costing you more money.

I also recommend to have spares for all your bedding in the supply closet, in case of damage you have replacements on hand and can avoid having to reorder/restock one of all your bedding supplies. The most common causes of bedding damages are oil stains, make up stains, and burn holes. When you do a damage claim in Airbnb's "Resolution Center," you will have to select the price of the replacement, and if you have it on hand, it is an easy way to get reimbursed quickly for the damage, and it saves the headache of re-ordering one of everything.

I recommend to wash all the sheets and duvets together, and then the towels and bathmats together. If you mix towels with sheets, you can expect a fair amount of lint on your sheets. If this happens, re-wash your sheets with detergent and baking soda, and then dry them with a few dryer sheets to help release the lint. As a last resort you can also use a lint roller.

Bathroom: A sparkling clean bathroom is so important for running a successful Airbnb. As there are very few items going into the bathroom, each one is very important. A decorative, refillable hand soap dispenser, good quality shampoo, conditioner, body wash, good looking bath mats and shower curtain, and color coordinated hand towels. I like to use bath mats from Ikea, they have grey and beige options I like to use, among a few other colors. It is a soft, velvety shag mat, washes very easily with towels, and is very durable and long lasting. They make a large and small rectangle size (Large Size: "Toftbo," Small Size: "Badaren"). If you choose to use bathmats with a rubber bottom, after a few dryer cycles the rubber will deteriorate and can look shabby. A fake plant or decorative item on the bathroom sink is a nice touch.

You can purchase large, pump style bottles of shampoo and conditioner at Costco or online. We like to use Tresemme as it has a salon style bottle, good reputation, comes in a large size, and is affordable and available at Costco in bulk. Using a large, pump style body wash is also a great option opposed to giving a new bar soap to each guest, which will be thrown away after their short stay at your place. You can also buy decorative, refillable pump bottles for your shampoos, label them, and then refill them as necessary. I like to have a colorful hand soap dispenser, a colorful hand towel and decorative fake plant, and then neutral bath mats and shower curtain. Having a super clean and decorative bathroom will add a lot of comfort to your guests, as we all enjoy relaxing and clean showers. I recommend Ikea, Amazon, and Wal-Mart for these items.

Kitchen: There are quite a few essentials for the kitchen, but how stocked you want to be is up to you. You will need a quality set of pots and pans, cooking utensils, eating utensils and plates/bowls/cups for a few extra people. For example, if you offer a space for 3 guests, you should have eating utensils for at least 4-5 people. A microwave, coffee maker, dish soap, hand soap, trash bags, clean sponge, knives, cutting board, cookie sheet, oven mits, and cooking essentials (oil, salt, pepper, spices, coffee, powdered creamer, sugar) are the basics. Adding additional cooking supplies like a toaster, hot water kettle, blender, mixing bowls, grater, whisk, etc are up to you. I like to fill out the kitchen the best I can, as many guests choose Airbnb instead of a hotel so they can cook at home. I recommend Ikea, dollar stores, Amazon, Goodwill, and Wal-Mart for these items.

Cleaning Supplies: Your method for purchasing cleaning supplies and stocking cleaning supplies is up to you. The basics would be a broom and dust pan, all purpose cleaner, rubber gloves, glass cleaner, cleaning rags, microfiber mop (washable head), and vacuum if you have carpets. Guests will often use these supplies to clean after themselves, especially during long term stays, so having them available under the kitchen sink or in a public storage closet is a good move, they may tidy up for you! You could also require your cleaners to bring their own supplies if you prefer not to stock lots of extra supplies. I use Mrs. Meyers natural cleaners, and advertise that I use non-toxic, chemical free supplies where available, but that is a personal choice and also a marketing tool. I recommend Wal-Mart, Amazon, and dollar stores for these items.

Setting Up the Locked Supply Closet: You will need an area to designate as your 'supply closet.' Here you will store extra toilet paper, paper towels, dish soap refill bottles, hand soap refill bottles, shampoos, conditioners, soaps, bedding sets, refill coffee, oil, salt, pepper, trash bags, cleaning supplies, kitchen sponges, air mattresses, anything you use to refill the supplies for your guests or things to keep safe and protected (air mattresses, extra bedding). I highly recommend to choose a closet, cabinet, garage (I keep items in bins with a tight lid to protect them from the elements in the garage), or storage area that is accessible by the cleaning team when they arrive to the home. If you do not lock this supply area, you can expect your guests to go through it and use whatever they like. Especially in American culture, traveling to a hotel or going on vacation puts us in the mindset of luxury, and we like to use all the towels we can, spoil ourselves in ridiculous abundance. I use a lock with numbers/letters so any cleaner can access it without needing a key. It is also recommended to keep an extra set of clean bedding here, in case bedding is damaged by guests or you have a cleaner emergency, you have a spare set available.

CHAPTER 4

Creating The Listing

Photography, Copy, Pricing, Calendar, House Manual, Pre-written Messages, Competition Research

Photography: Hiring a professional or semi-professional photographer with a fish eye/wide angle lens is one of the best investments you will make for your Airbnb business. IPhone's and regular digital SLR lenses do not capture the entire space in the photo. These photos can make a space look small and unattractive to potential guests. Blurry or dimly lit photos will not get you top dollar.

When doing your photo shoot, make sure the home is super clean, everything is set up beautifully – hand towels are folded nicely in the bathroom, duvet covers are on and stretched flat on the bed, kitchen is clean and not cluttered, bathrooms are spotless and have something decorative or colorful about them (grey empty bathrooms don't feel very welcoming). Open all the windows, turn on every light, and do the photo shoot on a sunny day around mid-day. Doing it in the evening will not give your space a bright, warm feeling.

For a low budget photo shoot, you can put an ad on Craigslist for a photo student or cheaper photographer to come for a discounted rate, you will want to advertise that you require a wide angle/fish eye lens. Cost per home is around $100-$250 for a professional photographer to shoot and do a basic edit of the images for you, depending on your home's size. No need for studio lights as you'd like your photos to look realistic and accurate.

Airbnb also offers a professional photography service on their website in select areas where they have contracted photographers working with them. I have worked with one in Los Angeles and had a positive experience. The price is around $150-$250 depending on your homes size. You can get a free quote on their website for your listing, although from the time of the request for a photo shoot until they photograph it and load the images into your Airbnb listing, it could take 3-5 weeks.

Copy: Write an inviting description about your place, highlighting the best aspects of your home, neighborhood, and its unique characteristics. Central location, near specific tourist attractions, peaceful and quiet or isolated, large and spacious, cozy or sunny, private or a busy area, any attractive adjectives and statements you can make about your place to attract guests. In "The Space" area of the Airbnb listing, you can create a story about what its like to stay at your home. "You enter into our large and spacious, cozy living room with a large wrap around couch and large flat screen TV to enjoy a movie with friends. Our open and fully stocked kitchen is great for preparing your favorite meals, and our sunny and beautifully decorated bedrooms have comfortable beds to relax in and have a peaceful rest." In one part you are describing the attribute, and in the second you are suggesting it's benefit, and how it could be enjoyed by the guest during their stay.

Beginning Pricing: Pricing is an intricate game that you will catch onto with time. For your first week/weeks of rental, you will want to make the price lower than usual, to attract more people to book. This is because your home and listing do not have any reviews yet. Airbnb listings live and die by reviews. Each guest you host can leave a public review on your page and rate you by stars in a few categories, so you will want to do everything in your power to honestly represent your space in the listing. Showing glorious photos and then having a small crappy place will quickly get you bad reviews and Airbnb might even close down your listing. They even have a category that guests reviews you in that says "Accuracy of Listing."

At first you will lower the price, get some guests to book, and share with them that they will be your first guests. For example, "Hello Emily! We are so happy to host you. Indeed you will be our first guest (or you will be one of our first guests!), and we are looking forward to your feedback and tips about how we could make our space and guest experience even better. Please be in touch if you have any questions or issues, as we want to guarantee you have a five star experience in our home." Emily will probably be understanding and feel special for being a first, and that you care about her opinion and comfort. Once Emily's been in for a day or two, ask her how it's going. Once her reservation goes well and she has checked out, you can write her a message to ask how her stay was. If she says "Great!" then you can ask, "So glad to hear that Emily! Would you be up to leaving us a nice review about your experience? As you are our first guest, it would add so much to our listing. I will also leave you a 5 star right now! Thank you so much for staying with us and come back anytime! All the best, Lauren."

Setting the Price: First step will be to look for other apartments and listings in your area that are similar in guest count, amenities, space and comfort. If you have a 4 guest, 2 bedroom apartment, type in those credentials into the Airbnb filters, check the same amenities your place offers, and see what the comparative listings' price points are (weekend, holiday, and weekday prices). Read more below in the "Competition Research" section. Luxurious versions will be the high price point, and basic/run down places will be your low point. Check for similar listings all around you and see what the market is like for your place. This will also give you ideas of things you can add to make your place stand out. You can read the reviews of those similar places and check for local feedback, what guests are wanting but that place didn't have. If you don't have a washer/dryer for guests to use, make sure you look for listings that also don't have that, as that can be a valuable amenity that guests pay extra for. You will most likely want to charge more per night for holidays and weekends, with an average of $25-$50 extra per night. Over Christmas and New Years, you can aim super high! I was able to double and nearly triple my rate for some of those nights.

Smart Pricing: This is a feature and algorithm of Airbnb that will automatically set the price of your listing based on similar listings around you, the amenities you offer, your ratings/review scores, and the supply/demand for each date. If you are the last listing available and 10 people are searching, the price will automatically go up because there is more demand. If there is no one searching your area for a few days, Airbnb will drop it to the lowest minimum price you have specified to try to attract bookings for you.

I look to Smart Pricing for insight into supply and demand, but don't use it often or live by it, as it's suggestions are not reliable. Sometimes it will suggest $42/night, and sometimes $188/night for the same home. It is a computer recommendation so it may not factor in your great decorations or the special feeling of your place. It gives a rough market value for your space based on demand. When in the "Calendar", you can click on a series of days, and then click on "See Price Tips" which is located under the Smart Pricing box. Here you will see what they are recommending for each day. If you set the price within 5% of their recommendation, they claim to advertise your listing more and that you are more likely to get booked. Sometimes it is way too low or high for my comfort so I choose my prices based on my knowledge of the price points that have gotten me booked quickly in the past, and the price points I set that didn't attract anyone.

Calendar: The calendar is one of my favorite places on the Airbnb App. When you have launched your properties online, you can see day by day who is checking in, who is checking out, displayed as a daily feed. You can also click on each individual properties' calendar, set your prices by night, view your payouts, message guests, and stay up to date with your guests arrivals and departures, adjust your pricing for unbooked nights, and review your progress and success with occupancy rates.

House Manual: The house manual is a pre-written message that you send to your guests as instructions for their stay. I like to send it approximately 7-14 days before their arrival, but you could send it the day before if you prefer. The address, lockbox code, parking instructions, location of extra bedding/towels, how to use the TV or coffee maker, how to change the temperature, Wi-Fi, where to find alarm clocks, details about the laundry machines, and you can also request information from them like their estimated check in/check out times. It's worth investing the time to make a thorough house manual as it will dramatically reduce the amount of questions you need to answer while your guests are staying.

For example, you have not included TV instructions in your house manual, and you have an elderly couple staying in your place, desperate for the nightly news. You may have to give them a tutorial on the phone for half an hour, only to head over in person to get the TV on for them. If you wrote detailed TV instructions in your house manual, you can kindly refer them to the manual for the instructions, and let them know if they still have questions or concerns to contact you right away and you will do your best to sort the problem for them as soon as possible.

The same goes for any details or questions the guest is asking for – Where do I park? Where is the lockbox? I can't find it. Where is the BBQ? I don't see it. Any and all guest questions can be covered and soothed with a detailed, informative, up to date, descriptive house manual. The pre-written house manual is available in the "Saved Responses" area of your message center, simply click on the guests' message in your inbox, and see below the input text box, an icon that looks like a piece of paper with lines/text on it. Click on this, and you will find your library of "Saved", pre-written messages and responses, and the option to edit or create new messages. You will also include a copy of this in the back of your "Local Guide" binder, more details below in the "Location Guide/Binder" section.

Pre-Written Messages: In the "Saved Responses" message area of your hosting Airbnb App, you can pre-write any helpful messages that you send all the time. I LOVE this feature and highly recommend the time investment for writing informative, caring, clear, and universal messages to improve your speed, thoroughness, and communication capabilities with your guests.

For example, I often get early check in requests, but my cleaning team needs about 3 hours to clean, so the earliest check in I can ever offer is 2pm instead of 3pm. So I have a pre-written message I send to my guests when they request an early check in. "Hello! I'm so sorry but my cleaning team will not have the apartment ready until 2pm at the earliest. When they finish, I will contact you right away so you can check in. Feel free to come by and drop your luggage off anytime after 11:30am, just be sure to leave the keys in the lockbox so the cleaners can enter. Thanks!"

The same goes for review requests, "Hey! I hope you had a great stay at my place! Would you be up leaving a review about your experience? I will also leave a 5 star for your right now! Thanks!" You can also send a pre-written message when checking on your guests, "Hey! How is your stay going?", or when your guest makes a reservation, "We will be very happy to host you, thanks for booking with us! I'll send more details about check in and parking details closer to the date. Thanks!" With a touch of a few buttons, you can automate your common responses. I recommend you take the time to write these so they sound personal from you, not robotic or cold, absent of sentiment.

Competition Research: You have your Airbnb space and its time to furnish, decorate, visualize your successful space, and take steps to materialize this vision. It's time to check out your local competition, and see how you can maximize your place to compete, succeed, and set the price of your place accordingly.

The first step is to type in your neighborhood or city into Airbnb's "traveling" platform. Here you will enter your guest count, home type, how many beds, your amenities, facilities, neighborhood, and I would slide the price filter down to under $300/etc if applicable, as you don't want to search through the luxury mansion versions of your guest count. Do not fill in specific dates as you will not be able to see all the available listings around you. After filling in the filters, click search and see what places come up. You can also view the map version to check out your neighbors' listings. Next, do this search with only your guest count, so you can see the wide range of competition in your area.

Depending on your location, many listings will come up for you to research their marketing copy – How do they highlight the neighborhood? The location? Go into their listing and see how they describe the benefits of the location, you can use these tips and insights to highlight the location in your own listing.

Some listings will appear will be luxury versions of your place, and some under-furnished or unattractive. You will want to check out the listings that offer the same or similar bedroom/bed count/amenities, and see what they are charging per night. Check what amenities they offer, and learn from what their reviews say. For example, a review like: "It's so messed up there is no map to the bus stop, its so hard to find!" If you will also be advising your guests to use that bus line, have a map in your home for guests to reference. You can learn a lot about what guests want and need by looking at your competition's reviews. If your competition has a glorious backyard and personal laundry room, and you are offering an apartment with no yard and no laundry facilities, you may reduce the price of your place. By checking on your neighbors, you can evaluate the market around you.

Then you will want to check out your competitions calendar by clicking "Check Availability" and here you will see how they manage their pricing. By moving your cursor over the available days on the calendar you can see how the nightly prices differ. Informed Hosts will fluctuate their pricing for weekends, weekdays, holidays, and local events. Have the Super Bowl around the corner from you? Double or triple the price of those nights. You will see that your local competition is adjusting and changing their nightly price based on season, month, day and the local events calendar.

After reviewing the listings close to you and similar in amenities, you can choose to price your place lower to win over new reservations, in the same range, or slightly higher and glamp up your listing with fancier photos and décor to be a bit higher end than the local option. You can gain inspiration by seeing what listings around you are succeeding (their high review scores and lack of availability on their calendar. Note some people live in their space so their availability may not accurately reflect their success). Look at what these Hosts are doing, and what guests are asking for and not getting. You can provide a needed niche!

Location Guide and Binder: This is a binder or booklet you can keep in the living room for your Airbnb guests. It has a list of all the close by and walking distance attractions/restaurants, the local grocery stores, and the popular, recommended, amazing dining options around. I type in the location of my property on Google Maps and search Food and then "Popular." Here pops up all the local eating options that are popular. I then assemble these tips into a Word document, organizing them by categories, and writing a short description, the address, the distance from the house, and the phone number. You can also do this with attractions, surf board rentals, the library, hot air ballooning, popular tourist streets and neighborhoods, shopping areas or centers. The more the merrier! Guests will instantly feel how much you care about their trip and comfort.

If you are a true local to the neighborhood, do your guests the incredible service of compiling an extensive guide for them. It can make their trip 1000 times more special. This will also get you amazing reviews. On the last page of this binder, I include a version of the house manual, which is instructions for using everything in the house. When a guests writes with a question, you can kindly reply "Hello! Please check the last page of the Local Guide Binder on the bookshelf under the television, we have detailed instructions written their for your convenience. Please let me know if you have any additional questions or concerns with it. Thanks!" You have saved yourself an extensive tutorial with your guest on how to do something in the home. You can also go beyond the house manual, and give more detailed instructions like "What to do before you checkout" (like take out the trash!) or "What to do if you lose your key."

CHAPTER 5

Cleaners, Cleaning, Laundry Management

Correct Availability, Experience, Attention to Detail, Reliability, Communication, Laundry Capabilities.

Hiring Cleaners: This may or may not be the biggest challenge with your Airbnb. I have divided this section into two parts. 1. Is for the single host, who has only one place. 2. Is for the multi-unit host, running 2-6+ Airbnb's.

1. Single Unit Host Cleaner's Strategy

If you are a single unit host, you may be offering your backyard backhouse, a room in your own home, or a nearby place that is easy to manage yourself. You will be cleaning yourself, or employing a friend, partner, relative, or local cleaning professionals to help you out. Your needs are a pretty manageable, as you have 1-3 cleans per week depending on your guest's length of stay. I recommend you train a few friends and a few local cleaners on how to prepare your place in case you are unavailable. Your trained cleaners should know how to set up the bedding, where to put the towels, what supplies to check and refill, where the storage closet is, how to check for damages and what items to check to make sure they weren't stolen.

It is important to schedule your cleaners the best you can in advance. As you are not providing a full time job for your cleaners, you can expect that they may not always be available or totally reliable as they have other responsibilities and employment, therefore you will want to train multiple, part-time cleaners who can fill in last minute if needed. Often times you will get a last minute booking, and if you are unavailable, it could be stressful to find someone last minute to clean and prepare the place for your next guests.

Typical cleaning hours are between 11am-3pm, so your cleaners should be available during those hours, seven days a week. Experienced, professional, detailed cleaners are recommended - not everyone knows how to properly 'clean.' Fresh, clean bedding and a super clean bathroom are the most important focuses. You may want to have an extra bedding 'set' for each cleaner you are regularly using, so your cleaners can do the laundry on their off-time at home.

For example, perhaps it takes the cleaner 1.5 hours to clean and prepare your place, but it takes them 3 hours to clean and do two loads of laundry on-site (one load of bedding, one load of towels). Will you pay them $18/hour for 3 hours, a total of $54 to clean your place and hang around to wait for the laundry? Or will you pay them $27 for cleaning ($18/hour x 1.5 hours), and then $10 to do the laundry at home on their own time (total of $37)? They will probably enjoy doing laundry at home while cooking dinner or watching TV and getting paid for it. You could choose to pay a flat fee per clean, and have them hang around waiting for the laundry to be ready so you don't have to buy duplicate bedding sets, but this is not the most efficient route, as you would save money in the long run investing in extra bedding sets from the beginning ($54 versus $37 over and over, this will add up).

If you are always using different cleaners, it is recommended to give each of them a bedding set because you will save money in the long run, but also because it is more likely they can make themselves available last minute for 1-2 hours to clean, instead of 3-4 hours to do the laundry on-site as well. You also have the option of doing the laundry yourself and preparing it for them. They could pick up the clean bedding set from your home when they are on their way to clean, and drop off the dirty laundry when they finish. You could also drop it off to them or have it ready in the supply closet, there are many options here for saving money by doing the laundry yourself.

Cleaners usually work independently. They arrive and clean without seeing you or you checking their work before the guests check in, so it is important to train them properly and give them a detailed cleaning checklist so they don't forget anything. I check my new cleaners work the first 3-5 cleans, and if I find many errors and see that they are not able to follow the cleaning checklist properly, I search for a new cleaner. I have included a cleaning checklist template in this book.

When the cleaner first arrives, they check for the keys, and text you that they have arrived and they have the keys. Secondly, have them scan for stolen items and damages. You have a limited time window to report damages/missing items to Airbnb, so you will want to get photos from your cleaners and upload them right away to the "Resolution Center" in the Airbnb App, so you can be reimbursed by the guest with Airbnb's help. Then the cleaner will start the laundry, or not, and clean everything, with the final step of texting you when they leave, so you know its done and you can offer the guest an early check in since the place is ready!

2. Multi-Unit Host Cleaning Strategy, Running 2-6+ Airbnbs

This is my specialty. I have been running 3-6 Airbnbs since I began my Hosting journey, and have discovered a million ways to do and not do the cleaning system.

This is my Best Recommendation: Assuming that your Airbnb's are in the same city and similar neighborhood, you will want to hire a professional cleaner that has a staff of their own. My "Head Cleaner" has four or five girlfriends she has trained, and she brings 1 or 2 of them with her depending on how many cleans she has for the day. I require her to train them at least 5-8 times on a home before I allow her to send them to clean an apartment alone without her. She works as a head maid, managing her own team of cleaners, managing all the laundry and bedding sets, and paying them all individually from what I pay her. This is really, really, really the best way to run multi-units in the same area.

Cleaner Responsibilities: Your cleaner is more than a cleaner, they do many other tasks. They check for damages, take photos and send them to you immediately, look for stolen items (hair dryer, iron, ironing board), check for lost keys, check the bedding for damages and send photos, pick up trash around the property, alert you when supplies are low so you can re-stock, manage your supply closet, refill the supplies in the home, alert you when something is broken, they make the beds look hotel style, they set up extra air mattresses or couch beds when needed, alert you when the gardener or trash man didn't come, they might even meet handymen and show them around for you if they are there cleaning any way. You need cleaners with the ability to do more than just clean, they should be able to follow your instructions as well.

Benefits of a 'Head Cleaner' System: I have experimented with hiring cleaning companies for all my places or for individual apartments, hiring and training specific cleaners for specific apartments, training many cleaners on many apartments, using professional Airbnb cleaning services, paying my friends or acquaintances to work independently with my cleaning checklist or with me supervising, and my take away from years of success and failure is to hire a head cleaner. Let the head cleaner employ workers, train them, manage them, and be responsible for them. If you are able to give them enough jobs, they will make themselves available for you, and reliability is sorted because there are so many trained back up cleaners wanting work from you. They have now made their own little cleaning company with many employees that depend on this relationship with you. They don't want to loose your business, so they will make things happen for you.

I use universal bedding (the same for every place) for all my apartments, so I give my head cleaner 3 full bedding sets for 6 apartments, and she cycles them through and does all the laundry herself at home. Your head cleaner and some of the cleaners must have a car (for carrying lots of dirty bedding and cleaning supplies), and laundry machines at home. If they are paying to go do laundry at a Laundromat, they are loosing money and 2-3 hours just to do your laundry.

Some tips about other Cleaning Systems: If you hire an Airbnb specific cleaning company or cleaning team, know that they are doing many other cleans between 11am-3pm, and may breeze through your place without checking details or being thorough. They may tick all the boxes on the to do list, but may cut corners because they are on a super limited time frame. My "Professional Airbnb Cleaners" left towels wet, beds unchanged, were rather unavailable, 'forgot' to check for damages, all because they were racing to do so many apartments (not all mine) in just 4 hours. If you can find a reliable and top notch Airbnb cleaning service, congrats! You have alleviated a large responsibility from your plate.

If you choose to hire multiple cleaners that work separately, you will be constantly chasing them for availability. For example, Susan is free Thursdays and Fridays, Ellen only Wednesday-Friday, Sammy is free Sundays and Tuesdays, etc. etc. You will be balancing many peoples limited availabilities, and chasing to book them and map out your cleaning schedule. What if Ellen doesn't show up due to a personal emergency, and the others aren't free, and you are out of town? It happens. You may have to cancel the next reservation, potentially ruining someone's hard-earned vacation plans, and loose your Superhost status capabilities. What if your guest extends their stay for an additional day, and you need to rework Ellen's schedule last minute, but no one is free on such short notice? Your in a bind.

Cleaning Crews Availability and Training: You want to have a cohesive team of cleaners working together whom are able to cover for each other. By using the "head cleaner" system, you are eliminating a ton of work for yourself, creating jobs, and allowing someone else to handle details, schedules, stress, and the availability puzzle for you. You're also letting them be the boss and run their own business inside your business, potentially maximizing profits for themselves, and allowing them to create jobs for their friends or family.

Your cleaning crew will need to be available seven days a week, between 11am-3pm, or whatever your checkout/check in window of time is. I like to hire cleaners and check their work the first few times they clean, evaluating their natural inclination for detail. I have hired and let go so many cleaners because they do not clean to the standard I need to ensure my guests are happy. Believe it or not, everyone does not know how to clean, and you will want an experienced cleaner with an impeccable eye for detail. I give my cleaners a cleaning checklist, and require them to initial after every task is done. See the template in the book following this chapter.

Reliable Cleaners Create Easy Check in/Check outs: Hopefully after the initial hiring and training of your cleaners, you have secured a team of super talented and trustworthy cleaners that work independently. If not, your full time job is interviewing, training, and checking on your cleaners in training.

If you have a lockbox then check in and check outs can be very simple. First, you text your cleaner or have them text you, letting you know that they have arrived and started cleaning (their arrival will also let you know that the previous guest checked out and left the keys in the lockbox). A bit later you receive a text that they have finished cleaning and the place is ready. Now you can text your next guest and offer them an early check in if they desire since the place is ready. Later, you will message your new guest and confirm that they figured out the lockbox and have checked into your place ok.

This system is deleting the two hours that some Hosts put in driving to the property to check their maids work, and then waiting around for the guest to arrive at the supposed "arrival time" to hand off the keys. With the lock box system in place, I sit on my patio, drink tea, text away while my cleaners do the dirty work, and my lock boxes do my Host duties for me.

Cleaning Review Scores: Your cleaner's attention to detail is going to make your Airbnb succeed with fantastic cleaning review scores, or make your Airbnb fail with a few bad cleaning reviews. "There was hair in the tub! Hair on the sink! Ew gross!" Your cleaner can potentially destroy your business in one day if the guest leaves a bad enough review. You can definitely bounce back, but most likely you will feel a large dent in your pocket from this situation.

In the emergency situation that the guest is disgusted by the status of your place, you can usually bribe your guest with a partial or full refund in exchange for them not leaving you a review. Sometimes, super worth it and necessary. Once I had a guest find a used deodorant stick in the bed after my new "Professional Airbnb Cleaning Service" did not change the beds, just made them up. I gave the guest a full refund in exchange for her not leaving me a review. Refunds saved the day! The guest does have 14 days to leave a review, so you will have to tell them that you will issue the refund after the 14 day window is over. Since you have written this promise to them on Airbnb messenger, they should feel confident that they will definitely get the refund after 14 days, because Airbnb can hold you responsible for your promise. I can't say that Airbnb loves this bribing system, but so far they haven't commented or complained about it.

Your cleaners need to know and understand Airbnb's cleaning review score system, be extremely reliable, and understand that if they mess up and a guest leaves a bad review, they have lost their job and messed up your business. They have to really care about you and your business. I treat my cleaners with the utmost respect and appreciation, because my business is literally in their hands. If you want to drive over and check every home after every clean, then you are taking the responsibility out of the cleaners hands. But if you have many Airbnbs, logistically this could be impossible so having trustworthy, incredible cleaners is a preferable way to run your show. If you want to go do another job during the day, or relax at home with your dog and cook Indian food, you will need a good cleaner that works independently.

Cleaner Communications: Another important quality in your cleaner is their communication abilities. Does your cleaner take instructions and follow them? Can they stay in contact and keep you updated on their arrival, departure, supply needs, restocking needs, damages, issues at the house? They must write you these details asap and keep you in the loop, promptly sending photos of issues and problems, otherwise your guests will be the ones to tell you something is broken or missing, and it will be too late to charge the previous guest. If you find that your cleaner is not communicating, and your reviews and scores are going down because of the issues that could have been avoided if she would have communicated better, you can design a communication protocol for her to follow, or jump back into the full time sea of hiring and training (and firing) cleaners.

Cleaners, Duplicate Bedding Sets and Laundry: I have spoken extensively about laundry in the 'Set Up Bedding' section, please refer to it for detailed laundry logistics. In general, it can not be pronounced loud enough, you should invest in duplicate bedding sets and have your cleaners do the laundry at their house. This is a smooth, no hassle, proven system. You do not want to limit yourself by having a cleaner hang around for four hours waiting for laundry to be ready. They could have gone and cleaned another apartment for the same price (if you are paying them hourly), and then you pay a bit on top for them to do laundry at home. Instead you had one cleaner hanging around for four hours at one apartment, and had to hunt down another available cleaner to clean and hang around at another apartment, and you paid them all double to wait for the towels to dry. You do have the option of only providing a duplicate set of towels/hand towels/bathmats, and having them wash all the sheets/duvets/pillow cases on site, which is easily accomplished in a two hour window.

It's best to maximize the speed and efficiency of your cleaning team because availability and the cost of your cleaners are important factors when managing your Airbnb's cleaning needs. The less cleaners you have, the more jobs you can give them, so the more they will want to make themselves available to you. It is less people to manage, train and depend on, and a great communication system can be developed between you and your cleaners if you are working together regularly.

Cleaners Payment and Appreciation: As for payment, I like to pay per job. I experimented with hourly, but found that sometimes it's a quick clean, and sometimes it's a more extensive clean or set up, but it always balances out the same for the cleaner over time, and I don't have to worry about cleaners hanging around to get paid more. If I pay a flat rate of $60 to clean a one bedroom and do the laundry at home, sometimes it will take her 1.5 hours to clean and then an hour of laundry at home, sometimes it might take 3 hours to clean and set up and one hour of laundry at home, in general she is always making $15-$25 per hour.

The only issue here is that they may try to rush through the job since it's a flat rate, so you have to keep your standards high and regularly check their work, have them send you photos, and keep them responsible for errors. I charge my cleaners between $5-$10 per mistake I find when I check (I rarely ever charge unless its an obvious mistake like not leaving any bathmats or not cleaning out the refrigerator), so my cleaners are financially responsible for their standard of work. I also choose to pay my cleaners very well so they don't want to loose the job, they follow my instructions, stay reliable and make themselves available to me. It's a win-win, mutually beneficial relationship. I can not bare to spend another 2 months hiring, training, and firing cleaners who don't care about their work or my self-built business.

My head cleaner is an amazing woman that I love, so I treat her with deep appreciation and when she makes mistakes I am very easy on her, as I need her commitment, reliability, high standard of work, fantastic communication skills, and wonderful cleaner management abilities. My world would be so much harder without her, so if she forgets something I ask nicely to remember to do it in the future, and she does. If she didn't, I would have to take measures to ensure the house is cleaned properly for my guests, which may mean hiring a new cleaner or inflicting large financial penalties, or lowering her payment and paying a third party (usually a friend of mine) $20 to go over and check her work (it will take them 10-15 minute to check everything, but I pay them for their time of driving over, etc). Remember, no one is perfect, but when you give your cleaning team a checklist and ask them to do a final check, they are responsible for making sure all the things are done properly 95%-100% of the time.

In the past I have had to train and fire so many cleaners for so many reasons. Finding a hard working, reliable, highly detailed, intelligent, adaptable, great at following specific instructions, available cleaner is a miracle. I wish you the best for finding yours! When you have one, your job responsibility gets cut in half. Show them appreciation, respect, spoil them, treat them like queens and kings, they are part of the foundation of your successful business. Don't treat them bad or look down on them, they are keeping your business going by showing up and doing a great job.

Training Hosts and Co-hosts: Now you have your property all set up and its time to train some friends, dependable employees, co-workers, or a back up person in the event you are unavailable to do your Hosting duties or have an emergency. This co-host should know everything about the properties and the system. Where the supply closet is, what goes inside, who are the cleaners, what are their schedules and contact info, what does the listing say and promise to the guests, what handymen to call for what repairs, how to use the lockboxes and the location of the emergency back-up lock box, where and what is the bedding and how are the beds made and where do the towels go? They should know everything they need to clean the apartment themselves if there is a cleaner issue and no cleaners are available to come.

You also need to train them on the Airbnb App - what is the inbox/messaging system, how does the calendar work, what is your average pricing, how to write messages or use 'Saved Responses', how to make a claim on the Resolution Center, and how to alter and accept reservation alterations.

This is a lot of information, so you may want to make a reference manual for your co-hosts so they know what to do and what to say in the event of an issue. Sometimes I ask friends to cover for me by taking phone calls, and I alert my guests of the temporary change via Airbnb messenger. "Hello! I am going hiking on Tuesday and Wednesday and may be out of service area. If you have any pressing concerns, please call my local co-host Tom at ######, and he will assist you. I'll be back online on Thursday! Thanks so much and sorry for the inconvenience. Can you confirm that you've seen this message? Best, Lauren." It is important to confirm that the guest has received the message, otherwise they may be calling you over and over while you are offline, and when you return online, there is a disturbing situation and Airbnb is already involved. Some guests are not tech-savvy and don't read all the information you share with them.

Once you have confirmed with your guests that Tom will be taking care of them temporarily, Tom should check the App every so often, accept/decline guest reservations, address any guest messages that look urgent/emergency, and then take phone calls if guests have immediate issues. A lot of messages could wait 48 hours until I am back online. You can even ask Tom to write to your guests "Hi! Lauren is hiking and I am covering for her until Thursday. I'm not sure the answer to your question, but I will have her get back to you right away Thursday morning! Sorry for the inconvenience! Best, Tom."

You may not want to go offline if you have check in and check outs on these days, as there are many more variables for Tom to handle like if something is broken, the guest arrived early and didn't tell anyone and you need to politely ask them to leave and come back later, something is lost or a damage claim needs to be filed, bedding is missing and the cleaners don't have extra and new bedding needs to be immediately purchased, etc. Tom may not remember or know how to do these things or who to contact, and it could be a mess for your guests checking in. He would also have to be on top of the cleaners, making sure they showed up and set up the house correctly, or going to clean himself if they don't show up.

With reservation requests, you have 24 hours to respond or you are penalized in your "Response Rate" score. So technically, you can go offline for 23 hours, without incurring a penalty for being an unresponsive Host. Or you could pay Tom to peak in every 23 hours and accept/decline requests, based on your guest policies. For example, they want to have a birthday party at your place, but you say on your listing no parties or events. Tom would have to decline that for you. Most inquiries I accept, unless there is red flag in the message. Accepting guest reservations is completely up to you, and you should be comfortable and personally confident about each new guest you approve to host.

It is important to have someone with back up knowledge of your places and the protocol if you want to go offline or be hands off sometimes. I manage many Airbnb units, all owned by different clients, so the protocol for each place is different. Therefore, it is very challenging for me to train someone on every detail of my clients sensitivities, preferences, expectations, pet peeves, and the specific protocol for each guest issue. My strategy is to go offline for 23 hours at a time when I have no checkouts/check ins, and pay Tom $20 an hour to take phone calls and handle pressing guests issues while I'm out of the picture. I don't ask him to go into my Airbnb App or messenger, I handle that every 23 hours, but let him do the on-site, emergency tasks for my guests via receiving phone calls. I personally find it more stressful to trust Tom to do everything correctly while I'm offline, and risk him making a wrong move which could cause me to loose my clients or get a bad review from a frustrated guest. So I personally choose to alert my guests to call him with emergencies, and check my Airbnb messenger every 23 hours. I am a one man show except for my cleaners and handymen, but their may be an easy way in your business structure to share the reigns with another so you can disconnect in a stress-free way.

CHAPTER 6

Hosting

Guest communications: This includes answering questions, confirming reservations, messaging guests the house manual before their arrival, giving local dining and activity recommendations, and receiving phone calls and text messages.

Organizing Repairs: If your space is in an apartment building, this may involve calling the Property manager or Super to organize a convenient time for both the handyman and for the guest for the repair to be made. You may need to go on-site depending on the repair and the comfort level of your guests. If you are hosting a personally owned home or condo, you will need to curate a list of local, trustworthy, talented handymen and plumbers. Meeting, employing, training them on the units and where things are is important for a self-sustaining Airbnb. If your handyman knows your place and can be trusted to have the extra lockbox code, it simplifies your job to call him and send him over (check with your guests first if the timing is ok) to make quick, last minute, emergency repairs.

Hiring Gardeners and Managing Trash Day: If you are managing Airbnb's in personal homes, the grass and landscaping will need regular maintenance. If you will not be cutting the grass yourself, you will need to hire a gardener to work independently, coming by every week or two weeks to tidy the yard. You will also need to hire a neighbor, the gardener, or someone to stop by on trash days to put the cans in the street and to bring them back in. I have my gardener come on the day the bins go to the street, and he does this for me. I then have my cleaner bring the bins back in on her next clean there. I write on her schedule for those days (bring trash bins in). If you find yourself in a bind, you can always ask your guests to take the bins out for you. I can not recommend this, as most guests would prefer no responsibilities while at your place.

Managing Cleanings: As discussed in detail in the Cleaners section, cleaning is a complicated system if you have many Airbnb's. Hiring and training excellent cleaners is your first step. From there you will be creating the cleaners schedule. The date, name of the property, and guest count should be included so the cleaner knows how many guests to set up for (extra beds, towels, bedding, etc). Knowing your cleaners washer/dryer speed and location also helps you manage your cleaning team and bedding sets.

Bedding Inventory: Guests will some times destroy or take with them a wash cloth, hand towels, or bath towels. I have my cleaner always leave the same number of towels, so we know if some are missing, regardless of the guest count. I have her inspect the bedding while taking if off the bed, for unfixable stains (oil, permanent marker, make up, adhesive, burn holes). Bedding is very expensive because you need a lot of it, so staying on top of the inventory is important, otherwise you will be paying out of pocket regularly to replace unseen, damaged or missing bedding.

Managing Supplies, Re-stocking, Re-ordering: Depending on your space, you may have many supplies and materials to purchase regularly. Training your cleaners to alert you on re-stocking needs is a great plan. Buying toilet paper, paper towels, cleaning supplies, trash bags and laundry detergent in bulk and stocking it in the supply closet is recommended, if you can trust that your cleaner will not take supplies for themselves. You may also have to re-order bedding or furniture if things are damaged or broken.

Damage Reports: If your place is damaged in any way, you will want to immediately upload photos of the damage and make a claim in the Airbnb 'Resolution Center.' This must be done by the main hosts account/the Admin account, as a co-host can not request or send money. If you are not the Admin, and can not reach your main host or do not have their log in details to make the report yourself through their account, call Airbnb customer service immediately. You must report and claim the damage before the next guest arrives. This could be 3pm the same day, and maybe you received photos from your cleaner of the damage at noon. You are on a three hour time race to make contact with the necessary parties and claim the damage before it is too late. Airbnb wants to make the correct guest responsible, therefore they need the claim done before another guest checks in.

Host and Owner's Expenses: You may be running an Airbnb for a property owning Client, at your own house, or in an all-inclusive apartment building. The main expenses when setting up an Airbnb are the supplies, furniture, and then purchasing the recurring supplies. This can be an initial investment of anywhere from $1000-$10,000 depending on your style, what you already have, and the rent/mortgage of the property. Then you will need to pay for home repairs and the recurring expenses like utilities and guest supplies. Gas, electric, trash, internet, TV, Netflix, gardener, toilet paper, paper towels, laundry detergent, coffee and kitchen supplies, and cleaning supplies.

Airbnb Customer Service Communication: You will probably experience a guest issue where you're not sure what to do or how to handle the situation. One great thing about Airbnb is the call center, you can chat with a live person about your issues. These days, the standard Airbnb phone operator has limited knowledge. If you are requesting something they say they can not do, ask to be transferred to a 'Case Manager.' These are the folks that know the details of the website, rules, and can go into a reservation, make necessary changes for you, or call your guest and get things done for you.

At the beginning of my Airbnb career, everyone I spoke to knew everything I asked. Nowadays, particularly in the last year, the company has grown tremendously and I think they've hired a new fleet of more unskilled, unknowledgeable phone operators. I try to keep my patience as they claim things 'can't be done' or 'don't exist' – because I know they do, I've done it before. Always be polite! This is your business, your cash flow, your daily bread, and the kind of 'boss figure' in your life. Simply ask for a Case Manager, and be even more polite and grateful towards them. They can help you.

Managing Resolution Center Claims: The Resolution Center is where you or your guest make a claim for some kind of payment or refund request related to an issue or complaint. You can view this section in your Airbnb App or on the website. As a host, you are responsible for addressing your guests claims and complaints here, and also publishing your own damage reports.

Creating the Location Guide binder and House Manual: You can create a local guide and house manual that will do your job for you. Compile a list of all the local grocery stores, restaurants, activities and shopping nearby, and put it into a binder. On the last pages, assemble all the instructions for the house, like how to use the TV, thermostat, where the towels and alarm clocks are, or how to use the BBQ. Your guests will then be semi-self sustaining and not write you messages or call you for this info. They will be grateful to have the information at their fingertips, and you will be grateful for your extra personal time.

Setting Guest Policies: As the host you will be designing your operating system, but also your guest's experience and expectations. If you are managing the Airbnb solo for a hands-off client, or creating your own rules for your own place, you will need to specify in your listing what your policies are. No noise after 10pm? Specific quiet hours? No parties, events or pets? No late check in? Late check in allowed but you will not be available to help them after 11pm if they have an issue? Clearly setting the policies will ensure your guests have correct expectations. When guest expectations are not met, they like to leave bad reviews.

Upgrading the Space: After you've had your Airbnb for awhile, you may receive valuable guest feedback, or raise enough funds to take your place to the next level of luxury or comfort. You may want to add an amazing BBQ and patio furniture set, get new art for the walls, add decorative chairs or carpets, get more upscale bedding, there are endless upgrading possibilities. The host will upgrade and set up the new furnishings during the 11-3pm gap when guests checkout, on an unbooked day/night, or block the calendar to do the re-design. You will also want to photograph the upgrades immediately, post them on your listing, and up your pricing accordingly!

Setting the Pricing

Base Pricing: Pricing is a game and flow you will only get into with a little time, experience, competition research, and by checking in with Smart Pricing's tips. I review my calendar to change my pricing twice a week, seeing which days were booked and what gaps/available windows those bookings created, and I adjust my pricing accordingly. For example, I receive a new booking that creates a one night availability on each side. Because I have a high cleaning fee, I will dramatically lower the price of those two nights, to help them get booked and still be affordable.

Cleaning Fee: Setting the cleaning fee is up to you. You can charge exactly what you pay your cleaner, slightly more to receive more income or cover the cost of your cleaning supplies, or less and cover the cleaners fee in the booking price. You could also choose to have a higher price per night and no cleaning fee, paying the cleaner out of pocket.

Paying the Cleaners: It is important to set up a system with your cleaner, what day they will send their invoice, and what day you will pay them. I have my cleaner send the invoice Sunday night, and I leave her a check in my mailbox before Monday night. I also do PayPal and Venmo for her when I am out of town. Sometimes the schedule you made the cleaner does not reflect exactly what cleans were done. For example, perhaps mid-week you got two new reservations, and added those cleans for her with a casual text, or the guest extended their stay and the dates on the schedule of the clean are not accurate because you had to reschedule it. It can be challenging to keep up with what you owe who if you are running 5 apartments, and you had 3 different cleaners do a total of 18 cleans, many last minute or with date changes. Creating a manageable system of invoicing and payment with your cleaners will erase a lot of stress and mis-management of money.

Security Deposit: Setting this amount on your listing is up to you. It may seem intimidating to guests if there is a $400 security deposit, they may assume their card will be charged that upon booking and refunded at the end. In reality, Airbnb does not charge this at the time of booking, they only charge a portion of this if you make a damage claim in the Resolution

Center. For example, I make a claim for $200 against my guest for breaking my coffee table and TV. Airbnb accepts and validates my claim, they charge the guest $200 without asking them, because this $400 security deposit allows Airbnb to do so. I personally choose to put a $150 security deposit, as its not too high and not too low for either host or guest. Airbnb does offer loose, informal coverage for your place automatically, so you don't need to be too scared about damages not being covered. There is also affordable Airbnb host insurance you can buy separate for peace of mind. In my experience hosting for a few years, I have made maybe 10 damage reports, mostly for damaged sheets or missing plates/cups.

Extra Persons Fee: In your listing, you have the option to add an 'extra fee' for extra guests. For example, you rent your place for $100 per night for up to three guests. After three guests, you charge $10 per person, per night. If they have six guests, you will be receiving $130 per night during their stay. This allows you to cover additional utility costs, the place will probably be more messy because there were more people, you will have to use more bedding/towels, set up and purchase a folding bed or air mattress, which are all additional costs for you. These small details do add up quickly, as you have many people staying in your space and using the facilities.

The Airbnb Review System

Writing Reviews: First and foremost, if your guest had an issue during their stay (bug in the bed, sink not working, broken dining table, door handle fell off, not enough towels), any issue at all, even tiny, I recommend you DON'T ask them or mention anything about leaving a review. Chances are, they will mention the problem, exaggerate it, and maybe even try to get a partial refund for their 'inconvenience.' I have a very simple, pretty-fool proof method.

Problematic Guests: If your guest experienced any kind of issue during their stay, leave it alone. They are not your review target. No review is so much better than a negative review. People are merciless and may not know how it feels to run your own business that can live and die by reviews. They don't respect or understand the amount of variables you are juggling, and may slam you hard because of their sense of failed expectations.

Very Happy Guests: For guests that are ecstatic at checkout, "Hi! We just checked out and had the best trip ever! Thanks so much for opening your lovely home! We will definitely come back and stay with you again!," you will simply say "Thanks so much! I'm so happy you had a great time. Would you be up to leaving us a review about your experience? I will also leave you a 5 star review right now. Come back anytime! Thanks so much and safe travels."

Unknown Guests: After a non-problematic guest checks out, I always write them, "Hey! How was your stay with us?" In my experience, about 50-60% of people answer back. Many people check out, sign off Airbnb, and forget about you. If they do write back "It was incredible, we loved it!" – Follow the protocol for Very Happy Guests. If they say "Oh, it was fine," you could investigate further, but I recommend you only do so if you are VERY needy for more reviews. In this case, you would respond "Oh ok! Did you have a good time exploring Hollywood? Did you like the decorations of the house, was it comfortable for you?" This is a bit risky, because they could just jump to leaving all their 'helpful' or obnoxious criticisms as a review instead of writing you back personally. But they may reply "Oh the house wasn't so great, it was ok" or "It was an excellent house, just my grandma got sick so the trip wasn't as we had hoped." Here you will gain insight into their experience, and be able to guess if they had a good enough time to ask them to leave you a positive review. You are aiming for 5 stars for every review, 4 stars is not actually a positive review. So you want only the enthusiastic, highly pleased guests to review you. Guests who had an ok and good time will probably feel generous giving you 4 stars.

Host Review Wisdom: If a guest had an OK or underwhelming trip, don't ask for a review. One bad review can close down your listing or deter all future guests from booking. I recommend only asking for a review of their experience if they clearly stated that they loved the place.

Once I had a group of Grandmas on a girls week trip at my place, and after their stay they praised me and thanked me deeply for a fantastic stay. I then reached out and asked for a review, only to find they made a laundry list of every tiny detail of the place that wasn't perfect, in an exaggerated way ("The tub was so hard to enter! Its too tall! They desperately need a railing and handle bar to step into the tub! It is not safe to bathe here!"). I was so upset, but was able to laugh a little about their senior perspective complaints. I had personally met them, given them a tour, sat with them for an hour chatting and giving recommendations, they told me they loved the house, why would they jeopardize the business I work so hard to take care of and to build? Unless you are a home owner or small business owner, sometimes guests have no idea how hard it is to upkeep a property and run/manage your own small business, and are merciless with their criticism. Some people see the world as a cup half empty, and inviting them to share their opinion is a risky game.

CHAPTER 7

Set Up Supply Lists

This list is for homes with queen sized beds, a queen living room sleeping option (pull out couch or air mattress), a twin sized folding bed, bathroom, kitchen, and patio/BBQ area.

Living Room Furniture:

Sleeper Couch

Coffee table

Mirror/Paintings

End tables

Lamps

Carpets

TV - Cable, Roku, Netflix

TV Stand

Air mattress

Bedroom Furniture:

Queen mattresses

Queen bed frames

Bedside tables

Lamps

Decorations/candles/plants/books

TV's

Mirrors/Paintings

Hangers for closet

Dressers

Alarm clocks

General Furniture/Supplies:

Dining table

Dining chairs

Desk

Desk chair

Small globe for desk

Office holder for pens/envelopes/paperclips

Desk ornaments

Carpets

Door mats

Patio Furniture

BBQ

2 Lockboxes

Ironing board

Iron

Twin size folding bed

Large laundry bags

Laundry basket

Heaters

A/C units

Decorations:

Decorative Candle Sets

Fake plants

Succulent plants

Paintings

Large mirrors (one for each bedroom and living room)

Dining table and patio table center piece

Real plants for patio and house

Linens for Queen 1 Bedroom + Living Room Twin Folding Bed+ 1 Bathroom (Up to 3 Guests):

This is a list for having one full extra 'bedding set', plus one piece per item as a spare for the supply closet.

7 Bath towels (minimum - recommended 10)

4 Hand towels (minimum – recommended 6)

7 Beach towels

3 Bathmats (minimum)

3 Large shampoo, conditioner, body wash

1 Bubble bath (if you have a tub)

3 Queen sheet sets (minimum - fitted sheet, flat sheet, 2 pillow cases)

3 Duvet covers (comes with 2 pillow cases)

4 Pillows

Extra blankets (throws for the couch, alternative style blankets)

Decorative pillows (one for the bedroom bed, some for couch/loungers)

7 Washcloths (minimum – recommended 9)

1 Queen comforters

1 Twin comforter

Twin folding bed linens - (2 twin sheets sets, 2 duvets, pillow cases)

Linens for Queen 2 Bedroom+ Queen Living Room Sleeping Option+ Twin Folding Bed+ 2 Bathroom (Up to 7 Guests):

This is a list for having one full extra 'bedding set', plus one piece per item as a spare for the supply closet.

18 Bath towels (minimum - recommended 20)

8 Hand towels (minimum)

18 Beach towels

5 Bathmats (minimum)

8 Large shampoo, conditioner, body wash

2 Bubble bath (if you have tubs)

7 Queen sheet sets (minimum - fitted sheet, flat sheet, 2 pillow cases)

7 Duvet covers (comes with 2 pillow cases)

8 Pillows

Extra blankets (throws for the couch, alternative style blankets)

Decorative pillows (2 minimum - one for each bedroom bed, some for couch/loungers)

18 Washcloths (minimum – recommended 20)

3 Queen comforters

1 Twin comforter

Twin folding bed linens - (2 twin sheets sets, 2 duvets, pillow cases)

Kitchen:

Hot water kettle

Microwave

Coffee maker

Toaster

Wooden spoon/spatula/whisk/kitchen utensil set

Fork/spoon/knife set for 10 people

Knife/scissor block set

- Zip lock bags, aluminum foil, saran wrap, parchment paper
- Mixing bowls
- Dish drying rack
- Cookie sheets/bake ware
- Oven mits
- Dish rags
- Kitchen sponges
- Dish soap
- Dishwasher tabs
- Large and small trash bags
- Large coffee refill
- Coffee
- Powdered coffee creamer
- White and brown sugar
- Coffee filters
- Cooking oils
- Salt and pepper
- Basic spice set
- Set of 8-10 people plates, cups, bowls, coffee cups, glasses, wine glasses
- Wine bottle opener
- BBQ grill stuff - lighter fluid, long lighter, small grill, grill tongs/supplies/small grill
- Large dish soap refill

Tea

Large trash can

Placemats for table

Coasters

Bathroom (for 1 Bathroom):

Shower curtain

Shower curtain rings

Decorative refillable soap holder

Decorations - fake plants, knick knacks. Statues, succulents, books

Toilet brush

Plunger

Small trash can

Hair dryer

Cleaning Supplies:

Mop (suggested - microfiber)

Bucket

All purpose cleaners

Vacuum

Cleaning rags

Gloves

Glass cleaner

Spray bathroom cleaners

Broom and dust pan

Scrub brush/cleaning sponges

Large lint rollers

Laundry detergent

Refill supplies:

Toilet paper

Paper towels

Trash bags small and large

Coffee, oil, coffee filters, shampoos

Laundry detergent

CHAPTER 8

House Manual and Local Food Guide Example

The House Manual is a custom guide that you will send to your guests a few days before arrival.

House Manual Example (Lauren's Home – Hollywood House)

Hey!

Here is some helpful information for your stay!

ADDRESS/LOCATION

The address is XXX Xxxxx Avenue. The lockbox code is XXX, and it is on the front gate to the right of the pedestrian gate entrance. When you leave, please lock the doors and return the keys to the lockbox.

INTERNET

The internet network name is WelcomeWelcome and the password is Hollywood

LAUNDRY

You will see the laundry machines on the back patio in the left corner. If you'd like to use them, there is laundry soap under the kitchen sink.

COFFEE

You will find ground coffee with a pour-over, pour-over filters, sugar and powdered creamer to the left of the microwave. There is also instant coffee and a traditional coffee maker.

YOGA STUDIO

Walk around to the back of the house near the outdoor dining table and you will find the shaded yoga area.

PARKING

I'm very sorry, but there is only street parking. Please do not park in the driveway as that is only for the neighboring tenants.

ELECTRONICS

The TV can be turned on with the large remote, be sure it is in HDMI 2 input mode. The small remote controls the ROKU, where you can find Netflix and many other entertainment channels.

The thermostat can be found in the hallway near the kitchen door entrance, here you can adjust the central air to the temperature you desire.

We have an outdoor stereo system, you will find the controller outside on the patio to the left of the patio door. Bluetooth your phone or use the auxiliary cord to play tunes in the backyard.

CHECK IN/AMENITIES

Check in is after 3PM and check out is by 11AM. If you already know around what time you will be checking in and out, please send me a message and let me know. With this information I can coordinate early check in's and late check out's for you and other guests!

Bath towels can be found on the bathroom shelves Extra blankets and pillows can be found in the hallway linen closet. The black garbage cans (in the driveway) are for regular garbage. Recycling goes in the blue can.

THANK YOU!

If you have any issues or concerns during your stay, please contact me immediately. I am a dedicated host and want to ensure you have a wonderful holiday and experience. I'm on Airbnb messenger a few times a day, but texts/calls to XXX-XXX-XXXX is the best way to get an immediate response.

Thanks! Lauren

The Local Food Guide and Practical Information Guide: This is content you will create about the local neighborhood, as well as home-specific instructions that will allow your guests to enjoy your place and be self-sufficient. I suggest you print the Guide and create a binder, which can be left on the coffee table or on the TV stand for your guests to reference.

Airbnb Local Food Guide and Practical Information

Xxxxxx Xxxxx Road, Los Angeles, CA, 90038

*most are walking distance (0.2-1.25 miles)

Grocery Stores:

PAVILIONS

*slightly more expensive than the average grocery store.

Supermarket chain with standard groceries plus deli items.

Organic products · Produce, Sushi

727 N Vine St, Los Angeles, CA 90038

local.pavilions.com

(323) 461-4167

RALPHS

*average grocery store.

Standard Grocery Store · Produce, Meats

1233 N La Brea Ave, West Hollywood, CA 90038

ralphs.com

(323) 876-8790

SPROUTS

*upscale, health food, organic/vegetarian friendly grocery store. Specialty chain offering a range of natural & organic grocery items (most carry beer & wine).

915 N La Brea Ave, Los Angeles, CA 90038

sprouts.com

(323) 217-1642

TRADER JOE'S

*eclectic and tropical themed, healthy grocery store with a fun selection of unique products.

Grocery chain with a variety of signature items, plus produce, dairy & more (wine & beer).

Organic products · Great produce

7310 Santa Monica Blvd, West Hollywood, CA 90046

traderjoes.com

(323) 969-8048

Coffee Shops:

STIR CRAZY COFFEE SHOP

Coffee spot with local art on the walls offers sandwiches, pastries, a bottomless cup & free Wi-Fi.

Quick bite · Fast service · Hip

6903 Melrose Ave, Los Angeles, CA 90038

(323) 934-4656

STARBUCKS

Seattle-based coffeehouse chain known for its signature roasts, light bites and Wi-Fi availability.

Quick bite · Fast service · Hip

859 N Highland Ave, Los Angeles, CA 90038

starbucks.com

(323) 493-1868

Bakery:

DELISCIOUS COOKIES AND MILK

Unassuming bakery known for its specialty cookies.

829 N Highland Ave, Los Angeles, CA 90038

delusciouscookies.com

(323) 460-2370

Gourmet Sandwiches:

MENDOCINO FARMS

Creative gourmet sandwiches, soups & salads, made with local & seasonal ingredients.

Comfort food · Quick bite · Healthy options

7100 Santa Monica Blvd #195, West Hollywood, CA 90046

Located in: West Hollywood Gateway

mendocinofarms.com

(323) 512-2700

Cafes:

CALIFORNIA CHICKEN CAFE

Local counter-serve chain offering a menu of rotisserie chicken, wraps & salads, plus sides.

Comfort food · Quick bite · Fast service

6805 Melrose Ave, Los Angeles, CA 90038

californiachickencafe.com

(323) 935-5877

CAFÉ GRATITUDE LARCHMONT (Vegan/Vegetarian)

Vegan organic fare & smoothies with hippie-inspired names served in a casual interior or on a patio.

Comfort food · Small plates · Quick bite

639 N Larchmont Blvd, Los Angeles, CA 90004

cafegratitude.com

(323) 580-6383

BLU JAM CAFÉ

Bustling American cafe popular for sustainable, creative & Euro-accented breakfasts served all day.

Comfort food · Healthy options · Hip

7371 Melrose Ave, Los Angeles, CA 90046

blujamcafe.com

(323) 951-9191

Pizza:

PIZZERIA MOZZA

*very popular and well known gourmet pizza restaurant. They also have to-go/pick up.

Acclaimed wood-burning-oven pizzas & antipasti in busy digs.

Late-night food · Comfort food · Small plates

641 N Highland Ave, Los Angeles, CA 90036

la.pizzeriamozza.com // (323) 297-0101

Restaurants:

GRUB

Quirky twists on brunch & other American comfort fare served in a 1920s bungalow & on its airy patio.

Comfort food · Quick bite · Hip

911 Seward St, Los Angeles, CA 90038

grub-la.com

(323) 461-3663

LALA'S ARGENTINIAN GRILL

Argentine-style meats plus salads & pastas served in a comfortable interior or on an outdoor patio.

Late-night food · Happy hour drinks · Comfort food

7229 Melrose Ave, Los Angeles, CA 90046

lalasgrillonline.com

(323) 934-6838

THE CAT AND THE FIDDLE RESTAURANT AND PUB

Classic pub grub in a punk rock-influenced British bar, reborn from its original Hollywood location.

Happy hour food · Late-night food · Happy hour drinks

742 N Highland Ave, Los Angeles, CA 90038

thecatandfiddle.com

(323) 468-3800

PETIT TROIS

Cozy spot with Parisian flare offers classic French fare & full bar from the team behind Trois Mec.

Late-night food · Comfort food · Small plates

718 N Highland Ave, Los Angeles, CA 90038

petittrois.com

(323) 468-8916

Quick Bites:

TA-EEM GRILL (Kosher)

*excellent Mediterranean food. Plates are more than enough for two to share. Customize your sides at the counter.

Offers falafel, shawarma & other Mediterranean & glatt kosher dishes for dine-in & delivery.

Late-night food · Small plates · Quick bite

7422 Melrose Ave, Los Angeles, CA 90046

ta-eemgrillinc.com

(323) 944-0013

PINKS HOT DOGS

*Can be quick or can have a long line – iconic L.A. hot dog stand

Creatively topped dogs (some for celebrities) draw long lines at this historic roadside spot.

Late-night food · Comfort food · Quick bite

709 N La Brea Ave, Los Angeles, CA 90038

pinkshollywood.com // (323) 931-4223

CHIPOTLE

Fast-food chain offering Mexican fare, including design-your-own burritos, tacos & bowls.

Comfort food · Quick bite · Hip

7101 Melrose Ave, Los Angeles, CA 90038

chipotle.com

(323) 297-0334

Upscale Dining:

PROVIDENCE

Chef Michael Cimarusti's fine-dining destination delivers innovative seafood in a tranquil setting.

Hip · Quiet · Great dessert

5955 Melrose Ave, Los Angeles, CA 90038

providencela.com

(323) 460-4170

House Manual and Practical Information

Xxxxxxx Xxxxxx Road, Los Angeles, CA, 90038

TV Instructions

The TV can be turned on with the large remote, be sure it is in HDMI 2 input mode. The small remote controls the ROKU, where you can find Netflix and many other entertainment channels.

Thermostat Information

The thermostat can be found in the hallway near the kitchen door entrance, here you can adjust the central air to the temperature you desire.

Internet

Network Name: WelcomeWelcome

Password: Hollywood

Alarm Clocks

Alarm clocks are available in the top drawer of the dressers.

Bath Towels, Extra Bedding, Extra Twin Folding Bed Locations

There are bath towels, extra blankets, and pillows in the linen closet at the end of the hallway.

There is a twin sized folding bed in the dining room closet with clean bedding next to it on the shelf. Feel free to set it up wherever you like, in the living room or one of the bedrooms.

Outdoor Yoga Studio

Walk around to the back of the house near the outdoor dining table and you will find the shaded yoga area.

BBQ Grill

There is a small BBQ grill outside next to the picnic table in the backyard. You will find lighter fluid, tongs, and a lighter in the kitchen. Please clean it off after your use, thanks!

Trash Cans

The black garbage cans (in the driveway) are for regular garbage. Recycling goes in the blue can.

CHAPTER 9

Cleaning Checklist

Airbnb Cleaning Checklist

Apartment:

Date:

Cleaner/s:

- Text the host that you have arrived, have the keys, and what time you started cleaning.

- Check for damages, check for iron, ironing board, TV remotes, sheets/towels. Send photos of damage and text the host a list of any missing items asap.

- Check under beds and drawers, cabinets and closets for left behind things. Text host photos asap. Keep valuable items on you, put non-valuable items in storage units.

- Dust all surfaces. Tables, TV stands, desks, counters, night stands above and below, windows, stove, mirrors.

- Vacuum all rooms, closets, carpets, under beds, and move large furniture to vacuum underneath.

- Mop all rooms, closets and bathrooms.

- Wipe down laundry machine, make sure there is no lint in dryer filter, no hair/dried soap on machine.

- Check the dining chairs for crumbs/stains.

- Sweep the patio.

- Look for any items that need to re-stocked. Text the host what new supplies are needed.

- Check that there is no hair on beds, toilets, bathtubs, in the drains.

- Water the plants.

- Vacuum the floors again after mopping if necessary.

- Move the furniture to clean behind and underneath (couches, beds, dressers, bedside tables).

- Dust on top of the fridge, window ledges, internet router, base boards, on top of water heater, laundry machines, top of dressers, top shelf in closets, top of paintings and mirrors on the walls.

- Clean under the kitchen sink and bathroom sink. Wipe down and re-organize cleaning products.

- Leave a clean mop there for guests to use (do not leave it brown and dirty for guests).

Linens:

- Wash laundry on fast cold/cold setting. Do not wash towels and sheets/duvets together. Keep an eye on laundry/set timers.

- Change duvet cover (every time)

- Check extra bedding in the linen closet if it is dirty of clean. Wash and replace in the closet.

- Put clean towels in the linen closet, in view. Do not put towels on the beds. Put the correct number of towels.

- While making the beds, check for hair/lint and lint roll each layer and the pillow cases.

- Make the beds look pretty. Duvet and comforter lay flat, flat sheet folded down so guest can easily get into the bed. Zipper of duvet at the end of the bed.

- Folding twin bed set up - Check the twin comforter for a clean twin duvet, clean pillow case/pillow, and clean fitted/flat sheet folded neatly in the closet next to the folding twin bed.

- Check the supply closet for clean extra bedding set ups/clean extra blankets.

Kitchen:

- Empty out fridge and freezer, wipe down inside.

- Check drawers and cabinets in kitchen that all kitchenware in clean. Check dishwasher.

- Do any dirty dishes and put away clean ones.

- Check that oven mit is still there and clean. If not, wash.

- Check there is enough dish soap in the kitchen. Refill as necessary.

- Check the kitchen sponge is clean. Replace as necessary.

- Throw away any left behind guest food or sugars, creamers, ketchup etc. Re-tidy the food storage area and clean shelves. Clean and minimal.

- Put one roll of paper towels in the kitchen. (Do not clean with paper towels).

- Wipe out the kitchen sink and clean the drain.

Bathroom:

- Clean bathrooms: bathtubs, showers, wipe down shower walls, bathtub walls, mirrors, sinks, toilets, sides and base of toilets. Check for hair in the drain and remove.

- Stock 4 rolls of toilet paper for the linen closet/under sink. Leave an extra toilet paper roll in view in the bathroom. Make sure edges are torn neatly and roll is at least ¼ full. If less, throw away.

- Check shampoo, conditioner, and body wash in showers. Wash off and close. Restock as necessary. Throw away left behind guest toiletries.

- Fold the hand towel in half and put one in each bathroom.

- Check the hand soaps in bathrooms, refill as necessary.

- Check there is no left over soaps or guest bath products in showers.

- Check the bathroom bathmats for footprints. Smooth out.

Trash:

- Empty all trash bins, replace with new bags. Wipe down trash bins for sticky/spilled food inside and outside, dust the lid.

- Take trash outside to the garbage cans.

- Pick up any trash in the driveway, on the side walk, on the porch, on the sides and back of the house.

- Take the trash and recycling bins out if it is their day. Bring them in if they are on the street.

Final Check:

- Do the final check, walking around the apartment to inspect all things.

  - All the beds are made and look nice, no tags sticking out or comforter is not flat?

- There is any visible hair on the floor, around the toilet, in the bathtub, in the shower?

- Any crumbs on the floors, couches, dining chairs, corners or coffee tables?

- Smudges on the mirrors or glass surfaces?

- Dishes put away from dishwasher?

- All dishes and cups clean and neatly arranged in the cabinets?

- Trash outside?

- Any trash left in trash cans?

- Any trash under the beds?

- Freezer and fridge are empty?

- Any laundry left in the machines?

- Side door is locked?

- Does it look, feel and smell clean?

- Are there crumbs or dirt on the floor?

- Send host a photo text of the bathrooms, bedrooms/made beds, the kitchen and living room.

- Send host a text message what time you finished.

Home Maintenance Tasks:

Cleaning windows, cleaning and re-arranging under the sinks, moving furniture and mopping underneath, re-stocking supplies and making lists of what you need, dusting base boards, dusting on top shelves of closets, mopping the patio, sweeping the driveway, cleaning spider webs from the patio and patio furniture, cleaning shelving in the kitchen, wiping down the chairs, checking BBQ and patio furniture, moving couches and vacuuming behind, etc. There are many maintenance tasks to be done every week.

ABOUT THE AUTHOR

Lauren Coats is a self-taught Airbnb Expert working out of California, Virginia, Brazil, and India. She is available for Hosting Mentorship, Consulting, and Full/Part Time Hosting. Visit her website www.magicbnbs.com, for more information.

Born and raised in Virginia, Lauren has traveled the world as a seeker of truth and lover of new cultures and experiences. Her Airbnb career began in Hollywood, California, where she set up and then managed six Airbnb's on her own. Her knowledge, expertise, and insight into the Airbnb platform comes from her own experimentation and experience, and all content in this book is her original creation.

Lauren loves dogs, her family, spontaneously jumping on a plane to a new country without a plan, beach living, healthy eating, anything Brazilian, spiritual wisdom and colorful art. She believes deeply in the power of traveling to heal the soul and mind. As one travels and see's new ways of living and thinking, the mind's conditioning cracks, and the soul is liberated into universal truth.

Printed in Great Britain
by Amazon